P9-DFU-515

Trey Parker, Matt Stone, and South Park

Other titles in the *Contemporary Cartoon Creators* series include:

Matt Groening and The Simpsons

Seth MacFarlane and Family Guy

Stephen Hillenburg and SpongeBob SquarePants

CONTEMPORARY
Cartoon Creators

Trey Parker, Matt Stone, and South Park

Adam Woog

San Diego, CA

For Mary Alice Tully, who first told me I needed to watch this show.

Printed in the United States

For more information, contact:
ReferencePoint Press, Inc.
PO Box 27779
San Diego, CA 92198
www. ReferencePointPress.com

LIBRARY OF CONGRESS CATALOGING-IN-PUBLICATION DATA

Woog, Adam.
Trey Parker, Matt Stone, and South Park / by Adam Woog.
pages cm. -- (Contemporary cartoon creators)
Includes bibliographical references and index.
ISBN-13: 978-1-60152-868-1 (hardback)
ISBN-10: 1-60152-868-X (hardback)
1. Parker, Trey, 1969- 2. Stone, Matt, 1971- 3. Animators--United States--Biography--Juvenile literature. I. Title.
NC1766.U52P37 2016
741.58092--dc23
[B]

2015003528

INTRODUCTION

Welcome to Trey and Matt's World

Trey Parker and Matt Stone, the mad geniuses behind *South Park*, are grown-ups. They have wives and children and everything. Despite these, as they cheerfully admit, the two are really just little kids inside grown-up bodies.

Or at least Parker and Stone remember what it can be like to be little kids. They know that, for children, the world can be many things—weird, puzzling, funny, interesting, frustrating, scary, satisfying—or some combination of these things. And life can be even stranger if the adults around them are erratic or eccentric.

The world of kids coping with the weirdness of life—based in part on their own childhood experiences—is what Parker and Stone explore in *South Park*, their outrageously funny and shocking cartoon series. Many commentators have noted that *South Park* excels at using humor to show how kids react to events and people around them. Journalist Carl Swanson comments, "The show . . . is bratty yet confident in its adolescent wonder at the strangeness of the world."[1]

South Park follows the fortunes of four elementary school students: Eric Cartman, Kyle Broflovski, Stan Marsh, and Kenny McCormick. The friends live in fictional South Park, Colorado, which is based on the real Colorado towns where Parker and Stone grew up. On the surface South Park seems like a typical bland community, but it is far from normal. The town instead is host to oddball characters and crazy events; its kids are often much saner, calmer, and more rational than the adults.

Rude + Funny + Satirical = *South Park*

At first Parker and Stone's show was notorious mainly for its bizarre plots and nonstop potty talk. Philosophy professor David R. Koepsell comments dryly, "No one has ever accused *South Park* of being the pinnacle of good taste."[2] Over time the series has continued to be funny and shocking, but it has also become deeper. Today *South Park* is as known for its incisive social commentary, typically about controversial topics like censorship, drug abuse, and religion, as for its weekly blizzards of foul language, rude jokes, and absurd situations.

Parker and Stone aim their satire at any and all targets, from government figures to celebrities and a wide range of ethnic groups. As a result, any given episode of *South Park* is guaranteed to insult someone, somewhere. But Parker and Stone have never backed down from asserting their right to do so. Stone comments, "If you're going to pull [an episode] off for offending somebody, you don't have any episodes of *South Park* left."[3]

> "No one has ever accused *South Park* of being the pinnacle of good taste."[2]
>
> —Philosophy professor David R. Koepsell.

An example of the duo's willingness to take on controversy dates from Season 18 in 2014. In one episode Cartman pretends that he is transgender (that is, he feels that he is a girl trapped in a boy's body). His reason is selfish: he wants to gain access to the girls' bathroom, which is nicer than the boys' bathroom. The situation soon becomes absurd and hilarious, but it also makes serious points about gender identity. The combination of humor and social commentary has made the show one of the most important satirical programs in broadcast history. Journalists Nick Gillespie and Jesse Walker comment, "Simply put . . . South Park has produced the sharpest satire of American politics and culture [on TV]."[4]

For Adults but About Kids

A show spoofing controversial issues like gender identity might seem an unlikely candidate for a hit series. And when *South Park* debuted in 1997, no one predicted that it would succeed. Parker and Stone assumed that it would last no more than a season or two. For one thing,

Trey Parker (right) and Matt Stone are known for the shocking and irreverent humor that characterizes South Park *and their other artistic projects. The pair seems in touch with both the childish and the insightful, making their comedy appealing to a broad audience.*

its audience was limited. Parker and Stone have always addressed an adult audience, not children, and many people (especially parents) consider the show suitable for adults only. In fact, it has a TV-MA rating, which means that the federal government has determined that the series is aimed at mature audiences.

But against all odds *South Park* was an instant hit and has thrived since. The program ended its eighteenth season in 2014, making it the third longest-running animated series in the United States (after *The Simpsons* and *Arthur*). It has also been honored many times by the entertainment industry: among *South Park*'s honors are five Primetime Emmy Awards, a Grammy, and an Oscar nomination. *South Park* also regularly appears on lists of the best television shows in history from such sources as the Writers Guild of America.

"Simply put . . . South Park has produced the sharpest satire of American politics and culture [on TV]."[4]

—Journalists Nick Gillespie and Jesse Walker.

Along the way Parker and Stone have become two of the most famous bad boys in the entertainment industry. They remain irreverent, mischievous kids at heart, but they are also rich celebrities with significant power in Hollywood. They have worked hard to get there, but they also have had a boatload of fun.

CHAPTER ONE

From Colorado to LA

Randolph Severn Parker III was born in Conifer, Colorado, on October 19, 1969. His nickname, Trey, is used in card games to mean "three"—he is the third generation Parker to be called Randolph Severn. The rest of his family includes his father, Randy, a government geologist; his mother, Sharon, an insurance saleswoman; and his older sister, Shelley. (If these names sound familiar, they should—they are also the names of Stan's family on *South Park*.)

Parker grew up in Conifer, about a forty-five-minute drive from Denver. The region around Conifer is mountainous, including a large basin west of the town called—what else?—South Park. As a young boy in Conifer, Parker liked studying science and martial arts. He also was shy. Parker later told a reporter, "I was extremely introverted except with good friends. It was all about math and science and tae kwan do."[5]

Parker, the Entertainer

This shyness began to evaporate when Parker's early interests gave way to another: the performing arts. But Parker was apparently not cut out to be a normal performer; even then his taste was for dark humor. At age eleven, for example, he wrote a sketch for his school's talent show called *The Dentist*. He later told TV host David Letterman, "I played the dentist, and I had my friend play a patient. It was sort of: 'What can go wrong at the dentist?' I just remember I had lots of fake blood and everything. Finally, [the patient's] head explodes. My parents got a call from the school; they were really upset. The kindergartners were all crying and freaking out."[6]

Parker's interest in the creative arts was cemented at age fourteen by a gift from his father: Randy Parker gave his son a video camera. Parker was fascinated with its ability to let him tell stories, and after that he spent almost every weekend making short movies with his friends.

During this period Parker also became increasingly fascinated with music, and he clearly demonstrated a serious gift for singing, music composition, and performance. He has remarked many times since then that all of these interests combined to make him into a "typical big-dream kid,"[7] hoping to someday make his mark as an entertainer.

A Future Star Is Born

Parker's interest in the performing arts continued into his middle- and high-school days. In particular, he developed a passion for Broadway-style musical theater, and by his teenage years he was regularly performing as an actor, musician, singer, composer, and writer. Notably, he almost always won a leading role in the theatrical productions his schools put on. For example, when he was fourteen he played the lead in his middle school's production of the musical *Grease*. And as a senior at Evergreen High, he was the student leader of the school's choir.

Parker's interest in theater reached beyond school. He also belonged to a community theater group called the Evergreen Players, in which he had the lead role in a number of productions. In addition he was a talented visual artist, designing sets for several theater projects.

> "In high school, Trey was a bit more shy but still well ahead creatively. It was clear he was going to do something."[8]
>
> —School friend David Goodman.

Parker also pursued creative interests outside school. For example, at seventeen he collaborated with a friend on a full-length album of original songs called *Immature: A Collection of Love Ballads for the '80s Man*. At one point Parker considered forming a rock band influenced by punk music's angry, confrontational style. David Goodman, a school friend who later became a *South Park* writer, recalls, "In high school, Trey was a bit more shy but still well ahead creatively. It was clear he was going to do something."[8]

Despite his busy schedule as a performer, Parker had time for other activities. He was a popular kid, evidenced by his election as prom king during his senior year. He got good grades. And he took part in another typical teenage activity: for a while he worked part-time at a Pizza Hut.

Stone, the Logician

Meanwhile, Parker's future partner in mischief was growing up in another Colorado town. Matthew Richard Stone was born on May 26, 1971, in Houston, Texas, to Gerald Stone Jr., an economics professor and textbook writer, and his wife, Sheila Belasco. (*South Park*'s Gerald and Sheila Broflovski, Kyle's parents, were later named after them.)

"I was going to become a logician. I read someplace that there were guys who made all this money doing high-level theoretical math for AT&T and I thought that sounded kind of glamorous."[9]

—Matt Stone.

Gerald Stone's career took the family to Colorado, so Matt and his younger sister, Rachel, grew up in Littleton, a suburb of Denver. Young Stone was always interested in movies, but his gifts were in math and science. He breezed through advanced science and math classes; for example, in sixth grade Stone took trigonometry at a local high school. By the time he entered Heritage High School, he was considered a genuine math prodigy.

It seemed inevitable that he was headed for a career involving mathematics. Stone later told a reporter, "I was going to become a logician. I read someplace that there were guys who made all this money doing high-level theoretical math for AT&T and I thought that sounded kind of glamorous."[9]

A self-described nerd, Stone rarely rebelled or got into trouble. His mother told a reporter that, if anything, his nerdiness was a little troubling. She recalls, "I'd say he was always a good kid. He did have one teacher in elementary school who said he wasn't reading the novels she had picked out during reading time. I asked what he was doing. She said he was reading the encyclopedia."[10]

As he grew older, Stone developed a philosophy of rejecting anything that he thought was trendy or widely accepted. For example, he wore Birkenstocks in high school—a type of sandals associated with nontraditional, hippie-like lifestyles. But he promptly got rid of them when he started college, simply because so many other students wore them. He later commented, "Everyone else had them and I realized that these people [wanted] to control my life. . . . I guess that defines my political philosophy. If anybody's telling me what I should do, then you've got to really convince me that it's worth doing."[11]

Getting to Know Each Other

After graduation both Parker and Stone attended the University of Colorado (UC) in Boulder. Their majors reflected their longtime interests: music for Parker and a double major in math and film for Stone. In 1989 both students were required to take a filmmaking class, and it was there that they met.

The two quickly became friends, sharing in particular a love of dark, outrageous humor. Specifically, they both loved a 1970s-era British TV show called *Monty Python's Flying Circus*, which was famous for its

The absurdist humor of British television show Monty Python's Flying Circus *influenced Parker and Stone's comedic outlook. In creating* South Park, *Parker and Stone also borrowed the paper cutout animation technique (shown here) of* Monty Python*'s American-born animator, Terry Gilliam.*

silly short skits. Punctuating these skits were bizarre animations by a American-born artist, Terry Gilliam. Gilliam's style for these cartoons was built around animated figures made from paper cutouts, a style that would later inspire *South Park*.

The Early Movies

In their film class, Parker and Stone began collaborating on various short comedies with titles like *First Date, Man on Mars,* and *Job Application*. (Like many of the partners' student movies, these can be seen on YouTube.) Parker and Stone shot a movie almost every week, and they teamed with two friends, Jason McHugh and Ian Hardin, to form a tiny production company, Avenging Conscience. (The name came from an early silent film by a legendary director, D.W. Griffith. According to some sources, the four students chose this name because they hated the film.)

Several of Avenging Conscience's movies mixed live action with a Monty Python–inspired cardboard-cutout animation technique. The group produced the animated portions of these films using only cardboard, glue, and an old eight-millimeter movie camera. Their figures "moved" using a technique called stop-motion photography. Stop-motion is a painstaking process that moves the cutouts in tiny, incremental stages, one frame at a time, in order to simulate motion when the film is played back at normal speed.

One example of these was *Giant Beavers of Southern Sri Lanka*, which parodied cheap-looking Godzilla monster movies made in Japan. Parker recalls, "It was sort of a Godzilla thing, but with a huge beaver. I had a little girl dressed in a beaver costume rampaging [through] a town."[12] McHugh later remarked that the movie was so ridiculous that it nearly got them laughed out of class.

A Milestone and an Award

Another animated film made in 1992 was a milestone for Parker and Stone: it was a direct predecessor to *South Park*. This early film was called *Jesus vs. Frosty*.

Like their other student productions, *Jesus vs. Frosty* looks incredibly crude by today's standards. But it is notable because it marked the

He's a Rebel

Parker and Stone have always enjoyed being contrarians—that is, taking on attitudes that go against other people's opinions, if only to provoke and annoy those people. This attitude stems from how the two were strongly influenced by the punk rock movement. Parker told a reporter,

> When you were a teenager in Colorado, the way to be a punk rocker was to rip on [presidents Ronald] Reagan and [George H.W.] Bush and what they were doing and talk about how everyone in Colorado's a redneck with a gun and all this stuff.
>
> Then we went to the University of Colorado at Boulder, and everyone there agreed with us. And we were like, "Well, that's not cool, everyone agrees with us." And then you get to Los Angeles. The only way you can be a punk in Los Angeles is go to a big party and go, "You can say what you want about George Bush, but you've got to admit, he's pretty smart." People are like, "What the [expletive] did he just say? Get him out of here!"

Quoted in Nick Gillespie and Jesse Walker, "*South Park* Libertarians," *Reason*, December 2006. http://reason.com.

first appearance of several things that would later become familiar to *South Park* viewers. These included early versions of Stan, Kyle, Kenny, and Eric as well as one of the show's trademark lines: "You know, I learned something today."

Jesus vs. Frosty is sometimes confusingly called *The Spirit of Christmas*, which was the title of a later film they made. As the title implies, this first movie pitted Jesus Christ against Frosty the Snowman in a deadly battle. By using these two iconic characters, it satirized how commercial aspects of Christmas overshadow the holiday's religious meaning. (Jesus wins by using his halo as a boomerang to cut off part of Frosty's head.)

Another animated short from 1992, *American History*, used the cutout technique to present the nation's evolution chiefly through its acts of genocide and conflict. This five-minute satirical narrative was good enough to earn the budding filmmakers a prestigious prize, the Student Academy Award. The Academy of Motion Picture Arts and Sciences—the same group that awards the Oscars—gives this prize annually at a ceremony in Los Angeles. *American History* beat out more serious-minded competition from respected college film departments such as the California Institute of the Arts.

Alferd Packer: The Musical

Encouraged by *American History*'s prize, Avenging Conscience embarked on a more ambitious project. This was a three-minute-long live-action fake trailer for a nonexistent movie musical titled *Alferd Packer: The Musical.*

The idea came from Parker's obsession with a bizarre figure in history: Alferd Packer, a gold prospector who was stranded in a snowbound Colorado pass with other prospectors over the winter of 1873–1874. To stay alive, Packer apparently ate some of his fellow prospectors, only to be tried and convicted of murder once he returned to civilization. The filmmakers chose this unlikely subject simply because they liked the idea of making a bright, happy musical based on a horrifying case of real-life cannibalism.

The production, like Parker and Stone's other output during this period, is crude. Though not an animated feature, it looks cheaply made (because it was), the editing is choppy, and the acting is amateurish. But it has flashes of their trademark biting wit. For example, Alferd Packer's horse is named Lianne in "honor" of Parker's former fiancée, his high school sweetheart Lianne Adamo. Parker and Adamo had broken up shortly before the group began work on the trailer, leaving Parker depressed and angry. (He later named Cartman's mother on *South Park* after Adamo as well.)

The fake trailer for *Alferd Packer: The Musical* was a hit with Parker and Stone's fellow film students. It was also a hit with Virgil Grillo, the chairman and founder of the university's film department. Grillo urged the young moviemakers to expand on their idea, making the full-length movie that the trailer allegedly advertised.

Making *Alferd Packer* a Reality

The partners took Grillo's advice. Parker wrote a script for a Broadway-style musical and composed ten original songs to go with it. Meanwhile, the two convinced their families and friends to invest a total of $125,000 in the project.

The ninety-minute movie was shot outdoors around Colorado's Loveland Pass in freezing weather late in the winter of 1992–1993. Using the pseudonym Juan Schwartz, Parker was the movie's star, director, and (with Stone) its coproducer. (Parker's father appears as the judge who sentences Packer to death.)

Upon completion, *Alferd Packer: The Musical* debuted at a movie theater in Boulder in October 1993. The audience, not surprisingly, was primarily made up of friends, family, and other students. In a mocking tribute to Hollywood tradition, the cast and crew, one by one, arrived at the theater by limousine and walked down a red carpet. The joke was that a single limo was picking all of them up individually around the corner and delivering them to the theater's entrance.

Sundance

The musical was a joke, of course, but the Avenging Conscience team took the film's fate seriously. Hoping to reach a wider audience, in 1994 they submitted *Alferd Packer: The Musical* to the Sundance Film Festival, a prestigious event held annually in Utah. They advertised it as "All Singing! All Dancing! All Flesh-Eating!"[13] and hoped that it would be accepted for an official screening there.

The Sundance organization apparently did not respond to their request, much less award them a screening. Undaunted, Parker, Stone, and their friends traveled to Utah for the festival, renting a hotel conference room and staging their own screenings. This garnered only a little attention from the public and media. Notably, MTV did a short news segment about the moviemakers, and Parker and Stone made some tenuous connections with established people in the movie industry.

The partners had hoped to sell the video rights to *Alferd Packer: The Musical* for $1 million. This optimistic plan did not succeed. Instead, a small distribution company called Troma Entertainment, which specialized in low-budget films, bought the movie's rights for a small sum

Trey Parker starred as gold prospector Alferd Packer in the 1993 low-budget Cannibal! The Musical. *Parker wrote and directed the black comedy, which failed to attract much attention upon its release but has since become a cult favorite among fans of Parker and Stone.*

and gave it a less obscure title: *Cannibal! The Musical.* But the film did not gain any attention until Parker and Stone became famous.

The disappointing sales of the movie were not the only negative aspects of the experience. Stone completed his studies at UC Boulder and earned a degree in math and film. But Parker was expelled from the university before he graduated because he had missed too many classes while working on the film.

Looking for a Break in Hollywood

On the other hand, one outcome of their experience would prove to be positive. Parker and Stone, convinced that they would be a success in Hollywood, moved to Los Angeles. Their partners in Avenging Conscience, McHugh and Hardin, decided not to join them.

Shortly after the move Parker and Stone met an influential film producer, Scott Rudin. Over a long career, Rudin has produced dozens of hit movies, including *Sleepy Hollow, The Truman Show, Zoolander, I Heart Huckabees,* and *Lemony Snicket's A Series of Unfortunate Events*. As a result of their connection with Rudin, Parker and Stone found a lawyer and an agent.

It seemed as though success might become a reality, but it was not to be, at least not immediately. Instead, the two spent several years trying to get a studio interested in their ideas. They lived in a succession of cheap apartments or slept on friends' couches, and they could afford to eat only one meal a day. Parker later commented about this period, "We were sleeping on floors thinking, Wow, another two weeks and we're going to be [expletive] rich. And pretty soon two weeks turns into two months, and two months turns into two years."[14]

The Boys Lose a Chance and Catch a Break

Parker and Stone invested most of their energy in pitching an animated children's program called *Time Warped*, which told fictional stories about figures in history. Over the course of a year the partners were able to create two pilot shows to illustrate their idea. One was about the biblical brothers Aaron and Moses; the other was a *Romeo and Juliet*–like story about two members of two extinct species, *Homo erectus* and *Australopithecus*, who fall in love despite their differences.

Parker and Stone hoped to sell *Time Warped* to the Fox Kids cable network. Fox did express some interest, but then the network disbanded its Fox Kids division before *Time Warped* could be approved. Fortunately, Parker and Stone piqued the interest of a Fox executive, Brian Graden. In 1995 Graden paid Parker and Stone out of his own pocket to produce *The Spirit of Christmas*, an animated video Christmas card that he could send to friends. *The Spirit of Christmas* was a slightly more sophisticated version of their early student film about Jesus and Frosty. (This second movie is sometimes referred to as *Jesus vs. Santa*.)

"We were sleeping on floors thinking, Wow, another two weeks and we're going to be [expletive] rich. And pretty soon two weeks turns into two months, and two months turns into two years."[14]

—Trey Parker.

Hardly Overnight Successes

Parker and Stone struggled for years in Hollywood to interest a studio in their work. For them, it was a time of near poverty and depressing failure, although they never gave up. Years later, after the two hit the jackpot in the entertainment industry, Stone gave a reporter his tongue-in-cheek "advice for success" in Hollywood:

> OK, here's what you do: Move to a new town with nobody except one or two friends, have no idea what you're going to do tomorrow, watch all your friends get jobs and get dental plans and health plans while you're sleeping on couches, give up any kind of relationship with anybody of the opposite sex, have no money and no security, have the faith of your parents tested. Do that for five years.

Steve Pond, "The *Playboy* Interview: Trey Parker and Matt Stone," *Playboy* (Kindle edition), June 2000.

As this title implies, the short featured an epic battle between Jesus and Santa Claus. It built on the characters of the first movie, early versions of Stan, Kyle, Cartman, and Kenny, and it introduced the town of South Park. (Later, in "A Very Crappy Christmas" during *South Park*'s fourth season, the boys try to make an animated short about the spirit of the holiday, using brief clips from the original short video.)

Going Viral

Graden liked *The Spirit of Christmas* and sent it out on videocassettes to about eighty friends. One of these friends digitized it and posted it online. It was instantly popular and is today considered one of the first videos to go viral.

Once its online presence skyrocketed, the cartoon began to get attention from the mainstream media. It won a Los Angeles Film Critics Association Award for best animation. And it got the partners' two feet in the door of the movie industry. Soon they were having multiple meetings a day with studio executives and were being offered various deals.

For example, Parker recalls that he was offered $1.5 million to direct a movie version of *Barney*, a children's TV show about a giant purple dinosaur that teaches lessons about friendship and manners. Parker recalls, "I said, 'Who the hell wants me to direct *Barney: The Movie*?' They said, 'They want it to be a G-rated thing, and they saw that you can make really funny stuff with kids since you did *The Spirit of Christmas*.'"[15] Not surprisingly given the syrupy subject matter, Parker turned the offer down, but another project did become a reality. A well-known filmmaker, David Zucker, had seen and enjoyed *Cannibal!* In 1996 he hired Parker and Stone to produce a fifteen-minute live-action film. He planned to show it at a party celebrating the sale of Universal Studios to a large conglomerate firm, Seagram's.

The result was *Your Studio and You*, a black-and-white short in the style of 1950s instructional videos. The intentionally earnest and sincere-sounding film purported to introduce the studio to the public. It featured brief appearances by a number of celebrities, including actor Sylvester Stallone (making fun of his dim-witted *Rocky* character), director James Cameron (as a handyman), and director Steven Spielberg (as a tour guide on a theme park attraction based on his own movie *Jaws*).

A billboard of Steven Spielberg displays his many film achievements. In 1996, the A-list director agreed to appear in Parker and Stone's Your Studio and You. *The funny industrial short marked Seagram's acquisition of Universal Studios, where Spielberg made such hits as* Jaws *and* E.T. the Extra-Terrestrial.

The Breakthrough

Your Studio and You is very funny, but it was nearly a disaster. Because of a mix-up in communication, Parker and Stone thought they would be directing a script that Zucker had already written. Meanwhile, Zucker thought they would be writing their own script.

By the time Parker and Stone discovered the problem, the day of the shooting had already arrived. In fact, some of the celebrities who were set to appear were already on their way to the studio. Parker and Stone had to write a script in about an hour and immediately jump into a frantic shooting and editing schedule. Parker comments, "That movie is as close to complete improv comedy as it gets. . . . You could probably make a feature film out of the experience of making that movie because it was just two dudes from college suddenly directing Steven Spielberg. We were up for six and a half days straight. It was the longest we'd ever gone without sleeping."[16]

> "You could probably make a feature film out of the experience of making *[Your Studio and You]* because it was just two dudes from college suddenly directing Steven Spielberg."[16]
>
> —Trey Parker.

The wit of *Your Studio and You* was popular with those who saw its premiere at the Seagram's party, and soon word about it spread throughout Hollywood. It proved to be the big breakthrough Parker and Stone had been fighting for. Their days of being just students obsessed with movies and rude humor were about to end.

CHAPTER TWO

Creating *South Park*

In the wake of the popularity of *The Spirit of Christmas* and *Your Studio and You*, Parker and Stone decided to focus their efforts on creating a full-blown animated series. Specifically, they wanted to develop the characters—Eric, Kyle, Stan, and Kenny—introduced in *The Spirit of Christmas*.

The first step was to decide on the tone and purpose of the show. They agreed that it would be satirical, irreverent, and outrageous, with a focus on current affairs. And they wanted to aim the show primarily at adults.

Developing the Characters

The first step was to round out the personalities of the kids, making them characters that spoke and acted in ways that Parker and Stone thought real boys spoke and acted—that is, not very politely. Parker comments,

> There's this whole thing out there about how kids are so innocent and pure. That's [expletive], man. Kids are malicious. They totally jump on any bandwagon and rip off the weak guy at any chance. They say whatever bad word they can think of. They are total bastards, but for some reason everyone has kids and forgets about what they were like when they were kids.[17]

Making the four boys realistic, to Parker and Stone, meant making them (at times) impulsive, self-focused, and cruel. This inclusion of less-than-perfect traits was especially true with Cartman, who is repugnant, foulmouthed, and bigoted. Parker and Stone have remarked that Cartman's obnoxiousness stems, at least in part, from themselves. Parker states, "He's both of our dark sides, [saying] the things we'd never say."[18]

Hard Truths

As part of their research, Parker and Stone studied established adult cartoon shows such as *The Simpsons*. They saw that it would be easier to explore controversial subjects, hostile attitudes, and morbid situations in cartoons than in live-action shows. Parker notes, "It might be hard to make live-action little kids dying funny. That would be difficult to do, even with special effects. But since it's a cartoon, we can control these kids in a way you never could with a real kid."[19]

Specifically, Parker and Stone made Cartman a character whose racist, sexist, and generally repellent opinions could be played for laughs. At first the partners worried that audiences would not ac-

Cartman, Stan, Butters, and Kyle (l-r) stand around the gravestone of their friend Kenny in a 1997 episode of South Park*. Parker and Stone strove to make the kids well-rounded characters, even Cartman who is known chiefly for his bigoted and otherwise offensive comments.*

cept such a character. But in the end they decided that it could work if his attitudes were connected to the naïveté of being an eight-year-old.

However, Parker and Stone also decided that the boys' personalities needed something beyond meanness. They were careful to let kindness occasionally surface, even in Cartman. This decision was made as Parker and Stone studied then-current cartoon programs. They realized that many shows, like *Ren and Stimpy*, featured harsh characters that did not reflect on their own actions or opinions. Parker and Stone concluded that viewers do not usually closely identify with completely negative personalities, so they decided that their show would be more powerful if they balanced the meanness with moments of compassion and, occasionally, insight. Parker notes, "There was some funny stuff on [these shows], but I could never get into it because it was like, 'Here is something [messed]-up, and here is something [messed]-up, and here is something [messed]-up.' But if you do something with a little heart and character . . . it sucks you in."[20]

> "If you do something with a little heart and character . . . it sucks you in."[20]
>
> —Trey Parker.

Distinct Personalities

Parker and Stone took care to give equally distinct personalities to the other characters. For instance, Kenny is a mystery: he wears his parka hood drawn so tightly that only his eyes are visible, and his voice is muffled to the point of near unintelligibility. Kenny has a hard home life. He comes from a poor family and has alcoholic parents—and often makes sarcastic remarks—but he can be sweet and empathetic.

Kenny is also the butt of a running joke: in the first six seasons he died a grisly death in every episode but came back the next week with no explanation. (In more recent seasons this happens only periodically.) Parker and Stone have supplied a couple of absurd explanations for this. In one episode Kenny has a superpower giving him the ability to come back to life. Furthermore, no one else remembers that he had died the week before, so they never wonder why he reappears. In another explanation, Kenny is not born again; instead, a new Kenny is born for each new episode.

Supporting Characters

As they developed their main characters, Parker and Stone also crafted distinct personalities for the supporting "actors." Among these were the kids' families, Chef (a school cafeteria worker), Butters and Wendy (other students), and Mr. Garrison (their teacher).

The adults on *South Park* have always been a little strange. For example, Mr. Garrison talks in class using his glove puppet. Stan's Uncle Jimbo is a disturbed gun fanatic. And Cartman's mom veers suddenly between being sweet and fiercely homophobic and racist.

In general, the adults on *South Park* are irrational, gullible, and not very bright. By comparison, the boys are reasonable and sensible, pointing out the absurdity of the adults' views. Philosophy professor Henry Jacoby notes, "People believe all kinds of things for all sorts of reasons; sadly, few pay attention to reasons that involve logic, argument, theory, or evidence. In this regard, the [adults] of South Park are no different."[21]

Although most of *South Park*'s main characters were developed during this period, Parker and Stone invented some later. For example, Terrance and Phillip, the stars of the boys' favorite TV show, were added in reaction to criticism that *South Park* was composed of nothing but crude bathroom humor and terrible animation. Parker and Stone retaliated by creating *The Terrance and Phillip Show* as a program within a program. Needless to say, *The Terrence and Phillip Show* is nothing *but* crude bathroom humor and terrible animation, humorously playing to the critics' complaints.

Striking a Deal

By the spring of 1996, Parker and Stone felt that they had a solid proposal and began pitching it to TV networks. Several were interested but passed for a variety of reasons. Notably, the Fox network again turned Parker and Stone down because *South Park* looked like it would be just too offensive to be funny.

The partners' proposal did attract two other cable networks, MTV and Comedy Central. But Parker and Stone were wary of the direction MTV wanted to take. They worried that their show might become a tamer program aimed at kids.

Disclaimer

Parker and Stone delight in satirizing everything and everyone. This includes themselves—they are not above making fun of their own work. For example, a tongue-in-cheek "health warning" at the beginning of each *South Park* episode announces, "All characters and events in this show—even those based on real people—are entirely fictional. All celebrity voices are impersonated . . . poorly. The following program contains coarse language and due to its content it should not be viewed by anyone."

Quoted in Wendy Rector Herrin, "Disclaimer and Theme Song," *Colorado Central*, June 1998. http://cozine.com.

So Parker and Stone went with Comedy Central. They liked Comedy Central's attitude, which did not back away from the adult-oriented aspects of the show. For example, the network was willing to accept the inclusion of Mr. Hankey, a talking piece of feces. Parker claims, "When we asked, 'How do you feel about talking poo?' they said, 'Love it!'"[22]

Comedy Central ordered only an initial pilot episode, which is standard procedure for testing a new show. Parker, Stone, and a small team of artists and technicians created the episode "Cartman Gets an Anal Probe" for about $300,000—a small budget for a half-hour animated show. They worked over the summer of 1996 at a facility called Celluloid Studios in Denver. They used essentially the same techniques as in the past, cardboard cutouts and stop-motion photography.

But *South Park* was nearly canceled before it aired. Comedy Central showed the pilot to a series of audiences to gauge their reactions before the show was broadcast nationally. The reports were disappointing; viewers—especially female viewers—generally did not like it.

But Comedy Central remained interested, mainly because Parker and Stone's Christmas videos were still growing virally online even months after the holiday season. So the cable company's executives commissioned five more episodes.

The Debut

Parker and Stone completed these before the show debuted on August 13, 1997. There was already considerable buzz among Comedy Central fans and others, and therefore anticipation was high. Still, writer Devin Leonard comments, "Nobody was prepared for what happened next."[23]

The show was an instant sensation. Many viewers felt that *South Park*'s sharp writing and up-to-the-minute satire made it the most important animated comedy since *The Simpsons*. And so *South Park* quickly became one of the most popular shows on cable television.

> "Most of the alleged humor on the premiere is self-conscious and self-congratulatory in its vulgarity."[24]
>
> —*Washington Post* TV critic Tom Shales.

The ratings numbers were impressive, ranging from 3.5 to 5.5 million viewers per episode, through its first season. And Parker and Stone made the covers of *Rolling Stone* and *Newsweek* magazines. Not surprisingly, Comedy Central quickly agreed to a second season.

Not everyone liked the program, of course; there was widespread condemnation from both the public and critics. For example, the *Washington Post*'s television critic Tom Shales sniffed, "Most of the alleged humor on the premiere is self-conscious and self-congratulatory in its vulgarity: [including] flatulence jokes . . . and a general air of malicious unpleasantness."[24]

Producing *South Park*

Whether their work was loved or hated, Parker and Stone had to use a time-consuming and tedious process to produce it. But their techniques steadily improved, and the show's success gave them a bigger budget to hire employees and buy sophisticated equipment. Thus, Parker and Stone dramatically shortened the amount of time they needed. They cut production time down from about three months (for the first episode) to one (for the rest of the first season). Today, instead of using physical cardboard cutouts and stop-motion photography, Parker and Stone's team of about seventy uses computer software programs to generate an episode in less than a week.

But even as the process has become more sophisticated, the show has kept its trademark crude look. As a result, current episodes look much the same as early ones. Parker and Stone do this because they feel that the show's simple look makes it funnier. Critic Stephanie Zacharek agrees, commenting, "Although the 'primitive' animation of *South Park* is supposedly a joke, it's really a secret weapon. The simplicity of Parker and Stone's technique is what makes it so effective."[25]

The Need for Speed

Producing an episode begins with Parker and Stone tossing around ideas, each contributing to this phase. Jason McHugh—one of Parker and Stone's Avenging Conscience partners, who also worked on *South Park* in its early days—comments, "Usually Trey is the starter and Matt's the chimer-inner. But together they will riff out and beat down a joke [until] it's even funnier than you ever could have imagined."[26]

Once the basic ideas are in place, the show's writing staff works collaboratively to draft a script, bouncing ideas off one another. Although what they write is funny, the work is difficult. *South Park*'s longtime executive producer Anne Garefino comments, "I think a huge misconception is that we sit around all day and laugh and get high. . . . We do one episode in one week and we work with pieces of the script at a time, it's really hard. We don't just sit around coming up with fart jokes."[27]

With a script more or less in place, *South Park*'s animators, editors, technicians, voice actors, and sound engineers go to work. They must be ready to accept last-second changes. By the following Wednesday—less than a week after the cycle begins—an episode is finished. It is then sent from *South Park*'s studios near Los Angeles to Comedy Central's headquarters in New York City for broadcast that evening. Sometimes, thanks to last-second changes, the show arrives just a few hours before airtime.

This lightning-fast schedule allows Parker and Stone to respond immediately to current news. For example, less than twenty-four hours after Barack Obama was declared the winner in his first run for the presidency in 2008, *South Park* aired an episode called "About Last Night . . ." that used portions of dialogue taken from Obama's actual victory speech. Another example was an up-to-the-second episode from 2014, "Go Fund Yourself," in which the boys form a com-

Co-executive producer Anne Garefino appears with Matt Stone and Trey Parker at the 2011 Tony Awards. Along with Stone and Parker, she has won five Primetime Emmy Awards for her work on South Park, *as well as a Tony Award and a Grammy Award for* The Book of Mormon *musical.*

pany called the Washington Redskins, satirizing a controversy over that football team's allegedly racist name.

A Terrible Work Ethic Makes the Shows Funnier

South Park's tight deadline serves another purpose as well. Parker and Stone think it forces them to be funnier. They feel that spending days perfecting a script destroys the humor. Garefino explains, "I think one of the reasons they do *South Park* at the last minute . . . is they always think they're going to find something funnier if they don't [finish it] until the very last minute."[28]

> "I think one of the reasons [Parker and Stone] do *South Park* at the last minute . . . is they always think they're going to find something funnier if they don't [finish it] until the very last minute."[28]
>
> —Colleague Anne Garefino.

The partners freely admit to having a terrible work ethic, avoiding projects until the last moment and then cramming everything into a final push. With perhaps a little exaggeration, Parker comments, "Given seven days to do something, we'll hang out for six, and then on that last day we will work harder and with more care than anyone in the [expletive] world."[29]

Despite the quick turnaround time, Parker and Stone have missed only one deadline. In October 2013, during Season 17, a power outage at *South Park*'s studios caused a delay of three hours. As a result, that week's episode could not air at its regular time. Parker told reporters, "It sucks to miss an air date but after all these years of tempting fate by delivering the show last minute, I guess it was bound to happen."[30]

Hearing Voices

In addition to the writing, a key part of producing the show is finding the right voice actors to bring life to the scripts. Parker and Stone still do most of the voice work. They handle most of the male characters, sometimes altering their voices electronically to make the pitch higher or lower. The show's regular females are voiced by a changing group of actors. And other actors are brought in to provide voices for supporting characters. For example, legendary soul singer Isaac Hayes played Chef, the school's now-retired cafeteria worker.

On occasion *South Park* staff members have also contributed voice work. For example, art director Adrien Beard is the voice of South Park Elementary School's only African American student, Token Black. (Reportedly, Beard was the only African American on staff when the character was created.) Furthermore, the children of employees often provide voices for very small kids, such as that of Kyle's babbling little brother, Ike.

Parker and Stone frequently ask celebrities to "appear," usually voicing themselves. These have included sportscaster Brent Musburger, actor Jennifer Aniston, comedians Cheech and Chong, and musicians Elton John, Korn, and Radiohead. Sometimes Parker and Stone ask celebrities to take on nonspeaking roles. For instance, comedian Jay Leno imitated a cat's meow and actor George Clooney

Cartman, Kyle, Stan, and Kenny (l-r) visit the mansion of Elton John in a 1998 episode of South Park. *John is just one of many celebrities who have voiced their own animated characters appearing in the show.*

gave voice to a barking dog. (Clooney, an early fan, was one of the people responsible for passing around the original *Spirit of Christmas* video.)

But plans for celebrity appearances do not always work out. For example, in 1997 comedian Jerry Seinfeld asked to participate. However, he and his agent reportedly changed their minds when the only role the comedian was offered was that of "Turkey #2" in a Thanksgiving special.

The Scientology Controversy

Another planned celebrity appearance turned into a worldwide controversy in 2005. Actor Tom Cruise had been scheduled to appear, but then Parker and Stone aired "Trapped in the Closet," an episode that mocked Scientology.

Scientology is a philosophy that its members call a religion. Members of the Church of Scientology believe, among other teachings, that humans are immortal but have forgotten their true natures—a condition that can be changed through an intense (and costly) regimen of spiritual rehabilitation. Scientology has attracted a number of high-profile members, including Cruise and fellow actor John Travolta.

In this episode, a group of Scientologists convinces Stan to join them. Stan is told he has to go through a series of expensive courses needed to restore his true nature. During these sessions an astonishing thing happens: Stan is told that he is the reincarnation of Scientology's founder, L. Ron Hubbard. Thousands of Scientologists (including Travolta and Cruise) descend on South Park to catch a glimpse of their reborn leader.

The episode sparked protests around the globe, and the Church of Scientology, which is notorious for bringing lawsuits against its critics, was furious. Not surprisingly, Cruise canceled his planned appearance. The episode also upset Isaac Hayes, a Scientologist and the voice of Chef. Until this point Parker and Stone had avoided mocking Scientology out of respect for Hayes. But when they did decide to take aim, the singer-actor resigned from the show, prompting Chef's retirement.

The First Muhammad Controversy

The Scientology episode caused considerable controversy, but it paled compared to the trouble Parker and Stone triggered when they targeted radical Muslims in two sets of back-to-back episodes.

The first of these sets stemmed from a controversy that erupted in 2005–2006. During that period a Danish newspaper artist had published editorial cartoons depicting the Prophet Muhammad, the holiest figure of Islam. According to strict interpretations of Islamic law, it is forbidden to show images of Muhammad. Radical Islamists were incensed at the perceived insult; riots broke out around the world, and the cartoonist was placed under a death sentence.

In 2006 Parker and Stone satirized this with the episodes "Cartoon Wars Part I" and "Cartoon Wars Part II." In them, Cartman tries to get the (real) animated sitcom *Family Guy* canceled by concocting a fake *Family Guy* episode featuring Muhammad. Cartman's hope was that threats from radical Islamists would force the show, which he hated, off the air.

Comedy Central agreed to air these episodes of *South Park* but insisted on censoring the scenes in which Muhammad appears. A black box replaced the holy figure's image, and some scenes were replaced entirely with title cards such as "In this shot, Muhammad hands a football helmet to *Family Guy*."[31] Meanwhile, all of the audio mentions of Muhammad's name were replaced with bleeps.

The shows attracted relatively little protest from the public at the time. According to Parker and Stone, the response from other animators was greater than the audience reaction. And they joked that they were not worried because they figured that *Family Guy* would be the target of any retaliation. Parker notes,

> When we did the Muhammad episode, we got flowers from the *Simpsons* people because we ripped on *Family Guy*. Then we got calls from the *King of the Hill* people saying, "You're doing God's work ripping on *Family Guy*."...
>
> We really weren't that brave. If [the *South Park* episode] did make it over to some obscure part of Pakistan, they'd be like, "Hey, we ought to kill the guys who did *Family Guy*."[32]

Inspiration from an Old Television Show

Much of the inspiration for *South Park*'s characters came from Parker's and Stone's own lives. But the two also drew on outside sources of inspiration. For instance, they studied a number of TV shows to analyze what worked and what did not.

One notable example of this was a TV sitcom from the 1970s called *All in the Family.* This show seems tame by today's standards, but it was highly controversial and groundbreaking in its day. *All in the Family* addressed issues such as homosexuality and racism long before other mainstream television shows took up such topics. *All in the Family* also had a number of characters unlike any seen before on TV. Of these, the most memorable was Archie Bunker, the blue-collar head of a family that included his liberal son-in-law. Archie was obnoxious, foulmouthed, sexist, and bigoted—but he was also funny.

Parker and Stone wanted to create a character like Archie on their show, one whose politically incorrect opinions could be played for laughs. At first they worried that modern audiences would not accept such a character. But in the end they decided that the character could work if he was an eight-year-old (and a cartoon to boot). Thus was born Eric Cartman.

The Second Muhammad Controversy

But Parker and Stone's second take on hard-line Islamists elicited a more threatening response. In another pair of back-to-back episodes from 2010, called simply "200" and "201," two hundred celebrities (all of whom Parker and Stone had spoofed in the past) threaten to sue the town of South Park over past insults. However, the leader of the protesters—Tom Cruise again!—promises to drop the lawsuit if the town can get Muhammad to meet with him. This happens thanks to a ridiculously complex plot that involves kidnapping the Prophet. All images of Muhammad were again blacked out, and references to him were bleeped.

Not surprisingly, the reaction was stormy. Notably, a radical Islamist organization, Revolution Muslim, posted online a warning that Parker and Stone risked death for their depiction of the Prophet. The group's website provided street addresses for Comedy Central's headquarters and South Park Studios so that protesters could find them.

In response, the New York City Police Department increased security at Comedy Central's headquarters in that city. In Southern California, South Park Studios' security was also beefed up. However, no incidents of violence were reported in either location.

At this point, for over a decade Parker and Stone had been creating a show that delighted or disgusted millions of people weekly. *South Park* was no longer a surprise hit; it was a solidly established hit. So Parker and Stone turned their energy and creativity to other endeavors as well.

CHAPTER THREE

Win Some, Lose Some

Even during *South Park*'s first season, as it became clear that the show was a hit, Parker and Stone had never thought that it could last beyond another year or two. So they decided early on to accept as many other offers of work as possible, not necessarily related to *South Park*. And even after the TV show became an established hit, Parker and Stone continued to take on a large number of these new projects.

Orgazmo

One early project was a low-budget feature film called *Orgazmo*. The partners had written and directed it before *South Park* debuted, fitting it between the shooting schedules for their unsuccessful *Time Warped* pilots. But for a variety of reasons *Orgazmo* was not released to the public until after the TV show debuted.

Orgazmo is a live-action comedy feature about an unworldly Mormon missionary (played by Parker) in Los Angeles who becomes ensnared in the pornographic movie industry, hoping to earn enough money to marry his sweetheart back in Utah. Stone also has a role in the movie as a dim-witted stagehand and photographer for porno films.

The movie garnered modest praise and attention when Parker and Stone screened it at the Toronto Film Festival, and a film distributor, October Films, purchased the rights to it for $1 million. *Orgazmo* was released in 1997, but it did poorly. One reason for this was that the Motion Picture Association of America (MPAA), which rates movies, gave it an NC-17 rating (meaning no one under seventeen was allowed into theaters). This naturally limited the size of the movie's potential audience.

Furthermore, the majority of reviewers thought that *Orgazmo* was just not very funny. One commentator was the prominent film critic

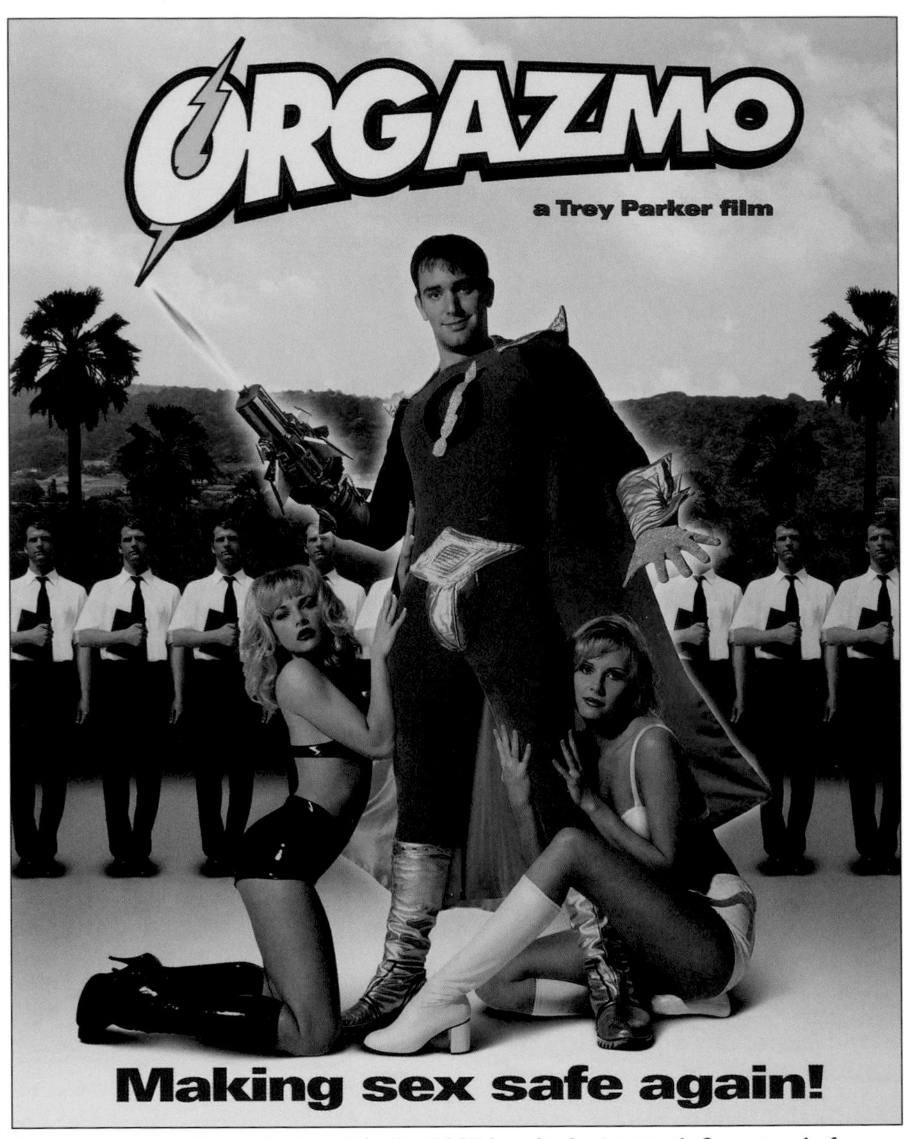

Trey Parker directed and starred in the 1997 low-budget comedy Orgazmo *before devoting his energies to developing the* South Park *series. The television show's demands on his time, however, have not stopped him from continuing to act in and direct feature films.*

Roger Ebert, who was a fan of *South Park* but not of *Orgazmo*. Writing in 1998 (about a year after *South Park*'s debut), Ebert stated that the movie was at best a feeble effort and not worthy of its creators' talents. He commented, "I guess 'Orgazmo' was a stage the boys had to go through."[33]

BASEketball

During this period Parker and Stone also had a hand in another project: a feature-length comedy called *BASEketball.* Although they had agreed to their role in this movie before *South Park* debuted, *BASEketball* was not made until after that date.

BASEketball is Parker and Stone's only major project that they have not primarily written and directed. The movie was written and directed by David Zucker, who had already made several well-received and wild comedies, including *Airplane!* and the *Naked Gun* series. Zucker was also Parker and Stone's friend; he was the person who had hired them to create *Your Studio and You*, the spoof of Universal Studios that had been a big boost to their careers.

BASEketball tells the story of two friends (played by Parker and Stone) who invent a game that is a combination of baseball and basketball. They make up crazy rules, mainly as a way to ensure that they win—the two are not good enough to play any other sport with serious athletes. Their game catches on, and thanks to a wealthy backer the two friends are able to create a professional-level BASEketball league. Meanwhile, they are forced to battle sinister team owners who want to change the game's rules and structure to their advantage.

"I guess 'Orgazmo' was a stage the boys had to go through."[33]

—Film critic Roger Ebert.

BASEketball was released in 1998 but, like *Orgazmo*, it was a critical and financial disappointment. (Later, in 2012, Parker and Stone made fun of it in the *South Park* episode "Sarcastaball.")

South Park: The Movie

According to the traditional rules of Hollywood, you are only as good as your last movie. Both *Orgazmo* and *BASEketball* were disappointments, and under normal circumstances Parker and Stone might have been finished in the film industry. But then *South Park* became a hit and everything changed: the two were now considered worthy of serious attention.

In particular, several studios approached them about making a feature-length movie based on their show. After intense negotiations, the partners came to an agreement with Paramount Studios for a project that they titled *South Park: Bigger, Longer & Uncut*. Work on its screenplay began while Parker and Stone were creating the second and third seasons of *South Park*.

The two had no interest in simply making a feature-length version of a typical *South Park* episode. It needed to be something special, something that would set it apart from the series. Stone commented at the time, "We would really rather not do the movie than have it kind of suck and be normal."[34] The solution: make it a full-fledged musical comedy. To this end, Parker wrote a dozen original songs for it in collaboration with a noted Broadway composer, Marc Shaiman.

As the story opens, Eric, Stan, Kyle, and Kenny sneak into an R-rated movie featuring their favorite TV characters, Terrance and Phillip, who specialize in bad words and worse behavior. After seeing the movie, the boys start cursing and misbehaving more than ever—even in front of their parents, which they had never done before. The parents, in their typically hysterical way, decide that Terrance and Phillip are corrupting their children. The adults then convince the US government that the solution is to go to war with the TV stars' home country, Canada.

Along the way, *South Park: Bigger, Longer & Uncut* makes fun of other feature-length animation, saving its strongest satire for inoffensive movies like Disney's *Beauty and the Beast*. And it carries on Parker and Stone's tradition of using famous actors in small roles. These include George Clooney (as Dr. Gouache, an incompetent doctor), Brent Spiner (who played Data on the *Star Trek: The Next Generation* television series and movies), and Eric Idle (a founding member of the filmmakers' beloved Monty Python troupe).

The movie's absurd plot let Parker and Stone comment satirically on a number of topics. They were able to make trenchant points on such subjects as censorship, "socially acceptable" behavior, and government suppression of creativity. Critic Zacharek comments about the movie, "At its most basic level, it's about the freedom and exhilaration of saying whatever you want."[35]

The movie is also gleefully vulgar. In fact, *South Park: Bigger, Longer & Uncut* holds the Guinness World Record for the most obscene words in an animated movie: 399. It also boasts 221 acts of violence and 128 obscene gestures, all in less than an hour and a half. Parker and Stone figured that this would earn the movie an R rating from

In the Studio

To create their television show, Parker and Stone and their crew spend long hours working in an environment of controlled chaos. Writer Steve Pond describes the interior of *South Park*'s production studios:

> Inside, the walls are painted in a Polynesian jungle decor, cardboard cutouts of the South Park characters hang over the cubicles, and the office that Parker and Stone share is an actual hut—a one room structure in a corner of the warehouse with stucco walls, a thatched roof and bamboo window frames. Amid a haphazard jumble of South Park merchandise, musical instruments and other paraphernalia of the creative life, the two gleefully profane (but decidedly moral) provocateurs go about the business of upsetting as many applecarts as they possibly can.

Steve Pond, "The *Playboy* Interview: Trey Parker and Matt Stone," *Playboy* (Kindle edition), June 2000.

the MPAA, meaning that no one under the age of seventeen could be admitted to the theater unless accompanied by an adult.

But Paramount's executives wanted to soften the movie, cutting some of the more outrageous scenes in order to make it PG-13. This much milder rating simply urges parental caution for anyone under thirteen, thus creating a bigger potential audience. Meanwhile, the MPAA wanted to give the movie a rating even stricter than the R rating Parker and Stone wanted. The organization insisted on making the movie NC-17, which would have meant that (as with *Orgazmo*) no one under seventeen could see it—and which would have resulted in a much smaller audience.

Fighting for the Rating

As the movie neared its release date, Parker and Stone continued to insist on an R rating. They refused to make the cuts that Paramount wanted, at the same time arguing that the movie did not deserve an

NC-17 rating. Parker and Stone won, but the issue was resolved only two weeks before the movie's premiere in June 1999.

In part because of the publicity surrounding this battle, *South Park: Bigger, Longer & Uncut* was a smash—audiences were curious to see what the fuss was about. The movie earned some $83 million at the box office—almost four times its budget—and much more from later DVD sales. It also received generally favorable reviews from critics. One such positive review came from the *Washington Post*'s Rita Kempley, who commented, "Although some will see this rude, crude comedy as the work of Satan himself, others will see the sharp, wildly funny social satire behind the profanity and potty jokes. . . . It's all in good dirty fun and in service of their pro-tolerance theme."[36]

"Although some will see this rude, crude comedy [*South Park: Bigger, Longer & Uncut*] as the work of Satan himself, others will see the sharp, wildly funny social satire behind the profanity and potty jokes."[36]

—Film critic Rita Kempley.

Adding to all of this was the fact that the movie was a contender for an Academy Award in 2000. Parker and Shaiman's song "Blame Canada" was nominated for Best Original Song. During the Oscar ceremony that year, actor and comedian Robin Williams performed a memorable version of "Blame Canada," complete with high-stepping female dancers dressed as naughty versions of the Mounties, Canada's national police force. Parker and Stone were in the audience, naturally, and they were dressed in gowns mimicking the ones that actresses Gwyneth Paltrow and Jennifer Lopez had worn to the ceremony the previous year.

That's My Bush!

The next project that Parker and Stone worked on during this period was a live-action television show. Produced for Comedy Central, it was a situation comedy about the president of the United States. The idea, the two said, was not to parody politics. Instead, Parker and Stone wanted to poke fun at the stereotypes of sitcoms, such as bad jokes, a laugh track, and such clichéd characters as a lovable but goofy lead, a long-suffering spouse, and a sassy maid.

A song from South Park: Bigger, Longer & Uncut *was nominated for an Oscar in 2000. Parker and Stone attended the ceremony in gowns and makeup, poking fun at the Academy Awards show's obsession with glamour and celebrity. Marc Shaiman, the songwriter, poses between the pair.*

The show took its cue from the 2000 US presidential election between Democrat Al Gore and Republican George W. Bush. Parker and Stone were sure that Gore would win, and they tentatively called it *Everybody Loves Al*. But the election proved to be extremely controversial, with an outcome so close that a Supreme Court ruling was needed to declare a winner.

In the end Bush prevailed, and the focus of the planned show, retitled *That's My Bush!*, shifted to him. This quick change from the political left to the right was a measure of Parker and Stone's neutral attitude toward politics. They have always insisted that they do not lean to one side or the other. Both conservatives and liberals have always been fair game for satire.

Parker and Stone had hoped to start shooting the program immediately after the inauguration early in 2001. But the lengthy process of deciding the election's outcome delayed them, and *That's My Bush!* did not air until April. The sitcom proved to be short-lived; the cost of producing it was relatively high, and audiences and critics generally panned it. Comedy Central canceled the series after only eight episodes.

Team America: World Police

In 2002 Parker and Stone began work on a much more successful project: a feature film called *Team America: World Police*. This was a political satire about an elite force of American soldiers who cluelessly destroy everything in their path while trying to stop terrorists.

Like all of the partners' work, *Team America* is a comedy with a serious point. In this case, they wanted to show that there are always dangerous or foolish extremists on any side of a conflict or issue. Parker comments, "The show is saying that there is a middle ground, that most of us actually live in this middle ground, and . . . actually this group isn't evil, that group isn't evil, and there's something to be worked out here."[37]

The film featured satirical versions of several real figures. Many were political leaders, such as dictators Saddam Hussein and Fidel Castro. But politics was not *Team America*'s only target. It also took aim at the entertainment industry by mocking big-budget action films and their huge explosions, elaborate chase scenes, and powerful superheroes. Also spoofed were a variety of entertainment celebrities, including, not surprisingly, Tom Cruise.

As with *South Park*, Parker and Stone contrasted the movie's satire with a deliberately crude and silly visual style. *Team America* did not use the familiar *South Park*–style cardboard cutouts. Instead, Parker and Stone used marionettes—puppets that are controlled from above

Parker, Stone, and Religion

Neither Parker nor Stone was raised in a religious household, and today they claim to be atheists. Nonetheless, both have always been fascinated by organized religion and (as evidenced by *The Book of Mormon*) have always tried to see the positive aspects of faith while not sparing their satirical drive. Stone comments,

> I think we've always had religion in the show[s] because it's just funny. I mean, there's just a lot of funny stuff. We've done stuff that's really anti-religion in some ways.
>
> But it's such an easy joke to go, "Look how stupid that is," and then stop right there. Religion's just much more fascinating than that to us. So from the very beginning, we always thought it was funny just to flip it on its ear and show how screwed up it is, but also how great it is. People couldn't tell if we were kidding.

Quoted in Nick Gillespie and Jesse Walker, "*South Park* Libertarians," *Reason*, December 2006. http://reason.com.

by strings and move in a corny, herky-jerky style. This was a tribute to two popular 1960s-era children's TV shows, *Fireball XL-5* and *Thunderbirds*, both of which had used marionettes.

Stressed Out

Reportedly, one of the reasons Parker and Stone used marionettes was that they wanted to avoid the problems of working with real actors, something they had experienced with *Orgazmo*, *BASEketball*, and *That's My Bush!* Even without live actors, however, the making of *Team America* was difficult and stressful.

For one thing, Parker and Stone were, as usual, operating under a very tight deadline. Also, the production was expensive; a crew of about two hundred people was needed for the excruciatingly slow process of making the "actors" move. It sometimes took half a day just to complete a single movement, such as having a character take a step or drink from a glass.

The pressure made the production of *Team America* a terrible experience for Parker and Stone. They frequently worked in twenty-hour stretches, consuming coffee by day and sleeping pills at night. Parker later commented about these long, difficult months, "I'm still having nightmares that I'm back on the set," to which Stone added, "I never want to have to work that hard again in my life."[38]

> "Do goofy stories [from organized religion] make people nice? What if, in their goofiness, these stories somehow inspire that in the right way? Is that a social good?"[41]
>
> —Matt Stone on the subject of religion in *The Book of Mormon.*

But production did finally wrap up, and *Team America* was released in October 2004. It received generally favorable reviews and made a modest profit. Predictably, the movie's targets condemned it, including North Korea's then-current dictator, Kim Jong Il. *Team America* was also severely criticized by the administration of George W. Bush—the same president lampooned by Parker and Stone's failed sitcom. The White House complained that *Team America* undermined American antiterrorist policy. A senior member of the Bush administration commented, "I really do not think terrorism is funny. . . . This is just unconscionable [unacceptable]. Not funny."[39]

The Book of Mormon

As if it was not enough to produce *Team America* and create weekly *South Park* episodes, during this period Parker and Stone began preliminary work on their most ambitious project yet, a Broadway musical comedy about the Mormon church. The subject matter—a serious religion that has millions of followers—might seem an unlikely topic for a musical comedy. But Parker and Stone have always enjoyed taking aim at religious faith, despite (or because of) a guarantee that criticism and condemnation will follow. Journalist David Itzkoff comments that the two "have a long history of tossing barbs at organized religion and having plenty more tossed back at them in return."[40]

The Book of Mormon *debuted on Broadway at New York's Eugene O'Neill Theater in 2011. The opening of the show set records in the theater's ticket sales, and backers recouped their $11.4 million investment in the first nine months of the show's run.*

Neither Parker nor Stone had been raised in a religious household; Stone claims that he did not know he was Jewish until he was sixteen, and Parker says that his parents unsuccessfully tried to raise him as a Buddhist. Today they insist that they do not believe in any religion. To them, any faith is just a made-up story.

At the same time, Parker and Stone admit that religion can be a force for good. They acknowledge that faith helps millions of people find comfort, and that it encourages them to lead positive, fulfilling lives. Stone wonders, "Do goofy stories make people nice? What if, in their goofiness, these stories somehow inspire that in the right way? Is that a social good?"[41]

The idea that "goofy stories make people nice" is one aspect of the partners' fascination with Mormonism. Their home state of Colorado has a large Mormon population, and as teens both were fascinated by how the Mormon faith seems to foster healthy family life. Parker recalls, "My first girlfriend was Mormon, and I went to experience family home evening at her house for the first time. 'What are you all doing?' 'We're sitting, and we're singing songs and playing games together.' I was like, 'Boy, that's [expletive] up. Families are not supposed to be doing that.'"[42]

Creating the Show

The Book of Mormon centers around two young, naive missionaries who have been assigned to spread Mormonism in the deeply troubled and desperately poor African nation of Uganda. (For young Mormons, missionary work is an important part of their faith.) Arriving after a long journey, the two are met by Ugandans who suddenly burst into song. The tune's melody is sprightly and cheerful—and completely at odds with the lyrics, which enumerate the famine, poverty, and AIDS epidemic that afflict Uganda.

As might be expected from Parker and Stone, this opening song is obscene and blasphemous, but with a serious theme: the Ugandans' heartbreaking conviction that God has turned his back on them. It sets the pace for the rest of the musical, which follows the young missionaries as their religious beliefs and optimistic views are severely tested.

As Parker and Stone worked out the story, they contacted two people they wanted to collaborate with: Marc Shaiman, who had helped write the songs for the *South Park* movie, and Robert Lopez, a seasoned Broadway writer-composer. As *Team America* wrapped up, Parker and Stone were able to devote more time and energy to their musical, and by 2006 they were flying regularly to New York to consult with Lopez and Shaiman. They also hired actors, dancers, choreographers, and technical crew members, holding workshops to iron out details of the planned show.

Another Opening, Another Show

Parker and Stone also enlisted Scott Rudin—whom they had met when they moved to Los Angeles—as the musical's executive producer. Rudin had originally planned to open *The Book of Mormon* off Broadway, which would have given its premiere a lower profile than if it had opened on Broadway, the center of the nation's live theater world. But as the show took shape, Rudin changed his mind and decided to take it directly to a high-profile theater.

One reason for this was that he was confident *The Book of Mormon* would be a hit. But there was another reason as well: the producer knew that Parker and Stone work best under pressure. Opening on Broadway would give the two no time to refine *The Book of Mormon* before a major audience saw it; the show had to work the first time out.

In addition to changing the venue, Rudin added pressure by quickening the pace of the production. The result was a hectic flurry of final rewrites, rehearsals, and previews just before opening night in March 2011. At the time Stone told a reporter, "It's crazy how fast it is. . . . Seriously, this is what blew my mind: We only heard the thing with a full orchestra six days before the first paying audience."[43]

The Payoff

The hard work proved worth it. *The Book of Mormon* was an instant sensation, drawing widespread critical praise and floods of enthusiastic audiences. And in the years since the show has shown no signs of slowing down. It still draws record audiences on Broadway. A cast recording became the highest-charting Broadway cast album in over forty years. Productions have been mounted in Chicago and London, and national touring groups have crisscrossed the nation. The musical has also won many honors, including nine Tony Awards (Broadway's equivalent of the Oscars) and a Grammy Award for Best Musical Theater Album. Furthermore, a film adaptation is in the works.

One reason for *The Book of Mormon*'s spectacular success, many observers have noted, is that it is not mean-spirited or cynical. At its core, the show has the same balance between biting satire and bighearted optimism that made *South Park* successful. Actor Josh Gad, who originated the role of one of the missionaries, remarks,

"It's about what can happen to a village in the most dire straits imaginable when they open their hearts up to believing in a higher purpose."[44]

Not all of Parker and Stone's earlier, non–*South Park* projects were nearly as successful as *The Book of Mormon*, either financially or artistically. Some were outright flops. But all of them have come from the partners' drive, artistic gifts, and staying power—characteristics that will likely stay with them as they look to the future.

CHAPTER FOUR

Now What?

Despite the ups and downs of their careers, today Parker and Stone are riding high. Long gone are the days of trying to stir up interest in a scandalous cartoon made with cardboard-cutout figures. There is a lot more going on.

The most visible aspect of their success is Important Studios, the production company they founded early in 2013. Important is headquartered in Culver City, near Los Angeles, and it oversees all of the partners' many ongoing projects. Parker and Stone sent out a typically cheeky press release announcing the studio's formation. They stated, "Having worked with several different studios over the years, we came to realize that our favorite people in the world are ourselves."[45]

> "In some ways it's a stupid comparison because [other artist-run studios like DreamWorks] are gargantuan. We want to be a smaller, more humble version of that. If DreamWorks is Walmart, we are over here knitting sweaters."[46]
>
> —Matt Stone.

Important Studios

Important Studios is unusual in that it is one of the very few artist-owned film/television studios in Hollywood—that is, one that is owned and operated by its creative forces rather than by people with a business background. The most prominent other examples of this in the movie industry are George Lucas's Lucasfilm and DreamWorks (which is co-owned by Steven Spielberg, David Geffen, and Jeffrey Katzenberg).

However, Parker and Stone are quick to point out how small their company is compared to such giants. Although the pair is relatively well known in Hollywood overall, Important Studios is still tiny by some standards. Stone comments, "In some ways it's a stupid comparison because they are gargantuan. We want to be a smaller, more humble version of that. If DreamWorks is Walmart, we are over here knitting sweaters."[46]

Using another analogy, Parker jokingly asserts that they are not very significant in the wider world of entertainment. There are many people, he insists, whose commentary and impact are far more noteworthy. He states, "You have to realize there are people who go on *The Tonight Show* because they have, like, the world's biggest potato. I like to think we're like the potato guys."[47]

As they have all along, the partners roughly split their duties at Important, although they stress that there is significant overlap. Together they are a formidable team—a well-balanced combination of artistic genius and hardheaded business. The ways in which they complement each other allow them to divide their work duties. Stone typically focuses on their company's business details, leaving Parker free to take his flights of creativity. Stone comments, "[Trey is] genuinely a true artist. I'm more mercurial. I have a temper more than Trey; I'm not proud of it, but I have that edge. Trey avoids conflict like the plague."[48]

> "I would not and could not do *South Park* without Matt. . . . I'm different around Matt than I am around my other friends, and we laugh at different stuff than we do with our other friends. And what we laugh about together, that becomes *South Park*."[51]
>
> —Trey Parker.

Parker remains the main creative and imaginative force. Stone, the one who excelled at logic and math as a kid, is more linear and grounded, and he is better suited to meeting real-world challenges than his sensitive friend. Toddy Walters, an ex-girlfriend of Parker who worked with him and Stone for several years, comments that Parker is still "just a big softy [with] a bit of anxiety about the world . . . who loves all sorts of music and musicals. I think Trey is supersensitive . . . and sometimes people like that need someone to be their backbone and have their back."[49]

The balance of their personalities has been a big reason why Parker and Stone have remained best friends for decades. By all accounts, they have also remained friends simply because they make each other laugh. Studio executive Jennifer Howell, who worked with Parker and Stone for years, comments, "From the beginning, everything they've

Parker and Stone in costume at a 2002 Halloween party in Los Angeles. Of their unique friendship, Parker has said, "I'm different around Matt than I am around my other friends, and we laugh at different stuff than we do with our other friends."

ever done was to one-up each other and make each other laugh. They have that great guy humor that starts when you're young: Make your friends laugh."[50] And Parker adds, "I would not and could not do *South Park* without Matt. I still can't put my finger on it, but it intrigues me. I'm different around Matt than I am around my other friends, and we laugh at different stuff than we do with our other friends. And what we laugh about together, that becomes *South Park*."[51]

"The Little Boy in Them"

It has often been pointed out that Parker and Stone are essentially still kids—or at least college students—who delight in getting a rise out of people by teasing unmercifully, often in mean ways. (According to legend, they have been known to break wind—or to say they do—on the lunches of *South Park* staffers who carelessly step out of the room.) On the other hand, they can also be kindhearted, and sometimes they take turns playing one role or the other. Their longtime colleague Anne Garefino notes,

> Matt goes for the jugular on everything; he has no fear. And Trey takes that and makes it sweet. [Or] Matt can sometimes be comforting, but not Trey.
>
> I remember once we were coming back from Vegas, and they'd rented a jet. I'm afraid of flying. There was this horrible turbulence; everybody was scared, it wasn't just me. It happened to be Trey's birthday. And he starts screaming, taunting God to kill us. "If you don't kill us on my birthday, God, you're a [expletive]." I'm crying and sort of laughing. . . . It's the little boy in them; that little boy is very much alive in them. The idea of teasing and taunting and doing those little outrageous things.

Quoted in Carl Swanson, "Latter-Day Saints," *New York*, March 7, 2011. http://nymag.com.

The two claim that they are so compatible that they rarely have serious fights about work or anything else. They further state that they would quit before seriously fighting over a project. Stone insists, "We never have had any big blowups, because we're big enough [expletives] that if we did, we'd never talk again."[52]

Toning It Down

In addition to the strong friendship they have developed over the years, and despite their hectic work schedule, Parker and Stone do have personal lives. Most of the details about the pair's private lives are just that—private. But a few specifics have emerged.

For example, in the years just after *South Park*'s debut and initial success, the partners suddenly found themselves famous and rich. What followed for both of them was a wild time of parties, lavish spending, illicit drugs, and general excess. During this period, not surprisingly, both Parker and Stone also kept up active love lives.

As they have grown older, however, they have cooled down. Both Parker and Stone are now family men with typical family responsibilities and relatively settled lives—at least as settled, perhaps, as workaholics and rich celebrities can be. Parker comments, "You can't work this hard and party at the same time."[53] Journalist Carl Swanson adds, "They're older now and have long since stopped bragging about their drug use and sexual conquests in the press. They became very famous very young and took it as an invitation to say and do pretty much what they pleased. But they're not flying to Vegas so often these days."[54]

Family Guys

For Stone, the settling down began in earnest in 2008 when he married a Comedy Central executive, Angela Howard. Today they have two children. Meanwhile, in 2006 Parker married his then-girlfriend Emma Sugiyama. (He serenaded the wedding guests with a set of songs written by pop balladeer Neil Diamond.)

But Parker's marriage ended within a few years, and he now lives with his partner Boogie Tillmon. They have a teenaged son from her previous relationship. In 2013 a pregnant Tillmon appeared in public, but details about the birth of a second child have remained private.

Both families live most of the time in Los Angeles, and both own lavish homes. For example, in 2013 Parker bought a seven-bedroom, twelve-bathroom mansion in Brentwood, a posh Los Angeles neighborhood, for nearly $14 million. But both he and Stone also own significant property elsewhere. For instance, Parker has houses or condominiums on the Hawaiian island of Kauai, in New York City, and in Seattle.

Furthermore, the two jointly built a deluxe ski chalet/Japanese-style teahouse in the ski resort of Steamboat Springs, Colorado. It serves as a winter retreat for themselves and Important Studios staffers. As a hobby, Parker designed some of the buildings they own. He comments, "I got into this little habit of architecture and building. I designed a house in Colorado and one in Hawaii. The idea is supposed to be build and sell—but then I can never bring myself to sell them."[55]

Enjoying Their Lives

Perhaps unsurprisingly, Parker and Stone very publicly enjoy their money and fame. (This can be seen as somewhat at odds with their disdain for celebrity.) But they are not at all ashamed or guilty about their status. Parker and Stone instead choose to hold themselves up as examples of how to achieve great lives. Furthermore, Parker told a reporter, he feels that it would be useless and hypocritical to deny or downplay the fact that he has a terrific time in life; he enjoys and appreciates his good fortune, and he sees it as a cause for hope. He comments,

> And yes, it's all about trying to dole that [good fortune] out to as many people as possible, but it's also about, when you have a great country, and it all works, and your life is awesome, then be able to say so! But for some reason, it's almost taboo to say, My [expletive] life is awesome, and I have a great time, and I have a sweet house and a nice car. . . . So, if you're not going to enjoy the dream, then there's no hope for anything.[56]

A Studio of Their Own

With money, their own studio, and settled home lives, Parker and Stone have created some major advantages for themselves within the entertainment world. Perhaps the most notable of these is their ability to raise money independently for a project.

Typically, a film production company teams up with a large studio to make a movie, with the studio providing financial and other backing. But Parker and Stone, with their own well-financed studio, need not rely on others for a project's budget. This in turn gives them near-complete control since no one else has a right to influence their decisions. In previous years, Stone recalls, talking to established stu-

Parker and Stone's mansion retreat in Steamboat Springs, Colorado. The $5 million home is made of reclaimed lumber and was built using eco-friendly construction practices. Visitors have noted that the home is quite lavish and contains no traces of South Park *memorabilia.*

dios about projects "was like meeting with Martians who were telling us that they were taking over and our way of life was basically over."[57]

Now, however, Parker and Stone are less pressured to comply with various demands, such as when Comedy Central censored the Muhammad episodes of *South Park*. Parker states,

> We've reached that level now where we're very comfortable saying, "You know what? We're done. We've made all the money we need, and we both have always had dreams of doing other things." As soon as they say, "We're not going to let you do a Muhammad episode," we can say, "All right, well, we're not going to do any more shows for you this season."[58]

Not surprisingly, this degree of control is tremendously satisfying to the partners. Parker and Stone can now do essentially what they want. This is undoubtedly thrilling to the duo, but perhaps less

Last-Minute Changes

Whereas other animated shows can take months to complete a single episode, Parker and Stone and their team rush to finish each *South Park* episode in less than a week. In this excerpt, journalist Devin Leonard describes the high-pressure atmosphere of the *South Park* writers' room on a typical day:

> Like college students, Parker and Stone can't seem to get anything done until the last minute. It's not that they aren't lazy. They are. But "South Park's" creators say this is the only way they know to be funny.
>
> People at South Park Studios . . . call the writers' room "the source of great joy or the source of great sorrow." This seems to be a sorrowful day. The show's creators are sitting at the room's long table, unshaven and tired-looking. Parker appears to be under a great deal of stress.
>
> It is a Monday afternoon in April, and they are rushing to finish an episode that will air Wednesday night. They have yet to come up with a first or last scene. The rest of the episode seems to be up in the air too. "I had a radical idea last night that totally changed the whole show," Parker says.
>
> It would be a disaster for any other animated series. You won't find "Simpsons" creator Matt Groening tearing apart his show at the last minute.

Devin Leonard, "'South Park' Creators Haven't Lost Their Edge," *Fortune*, October 27, 2006. http://archive.fortune.com.

so to others in the industry. The prospect of two of Hollywood's most famous bad boys doing as they please is one that Comedy Central executive Doug Herzog sums up by commenting, "Bringing money to the table goes a long way. Money talks. . . . Matt and Trey with a lot of money. Be afraid."[59]

South Park Abides

The projects that Parker and Stone develop and control through Important Studios are both large (such as movies) and small (such as T-shirts and video games). Among their planned large projects, for example, is a film version of *The Book of Mormon,* which is probably an inevitable development given the wild success of the live show.

Another planned project is an unlikely sounding collaboration with two musician friends: Les Claypool of the band Primus and Mickey Melchiondo, who was formerly the leader of the band Ween. Parker and Stone are hoping to produce a quirky reality-based fishing show for TV starring the musicians. Melchiondo says the series will combine the sport with music, comedy, and guest stars. He calls it "a fishing show that you do not have to be into fishing to enjoy."[60]

But the real direction of Parker and Stone's future work may be in new forms of media, beyond traditional TV, movies, and games. The *South Park* "brand" already performs spectacularly in these new areas. For example, the program dominates iTunes' top one hundred television show downloads. And Amp'd Mobile, a cellphone service provider, is in discussions to launch a 24/7 *South Park* channel for its customers.

> "Bringing money to the table goes a long way [in getting projects started in Hollywood]. Money talks. . . . Matt and Trey with a lot of money. Be afraid."[59]
>
> —Comedy Central executive Doug Herzog.

But despite these and other (mostly top-secret) Important Studios projects, Parker and Stone's most famous creation is still their first great success, *South Park*. For years after its debut, the show consistently maintained the highest ratings of any basic cable program. Figures in more recent years have fluctuated, but *South Park* remains one of Comedy Central's highest-rated shows. And the network has shown its faith in the duo by guaranteeing the series' contract at least through 2016, when it will be in its twentieth season.

It is likely, but not guaranteed, that the show will continue beyond this obligation. In public Parker and Stone have deliberately left the question open. They have stated many times that they will be happy to keep producing the program indefinitely. On the other hand, they also say that they will shut it down if they feel that they—and their characters—have nothing more to say. They have no interest, they say, in continuing just to be continuing. Parker comments, "When you're having success, you think about getting old. . . . I don't want to be that [expletive] old guy still trying to do [expletive] that's not working, you know? I want to go away before that, get a farm or something. It's so pathetic. There are a lot of people in this town [Los Angeles] who really should have left a while ago."[61]

Up and Down

Like all entertainers, performers, and other artists, Parker and Stone have had ups and downs in their careers. Whereas some of their projects have failed miserably, others have been huge successes. It is likely that this will continue to be true for their future projects, although they have come to realize that it all tends to even out.

A notable example concerned *South Park*'s performance in its first few years. It was a smash hit at the beginning, then dropped in the ratings, at which point some observers predicted that the duo's time had passed. (The critics were obviously wrong.) Parker and Stone's friend and fellow cartoonist Mike Judge, the creator of *Beavis and Butthead* and *King of the Hill*, gave the two some good advice about this phenomenon. Parker recalls, "He said, 'There's going to be this big rise, and then everyone will hate you. You just ride it out and do your job, and you're just a show.' And we're finally . . . leveled out. It's a good place to be, because there's not as much pressure. Once you go up and down, you realize it's all a bunch of [expletive]."[62]

Controversies

When it comes to *South Park* and their various other projects, Parker and Stone say that in the future they have absolutely no plans to give up one of their bedrock beliefs: that they should remain shamelessly outrageous, to the point of creating major controversies.

This includes continuing to be equal-opportunity offenders, refusing to take sides on an issue, and insisting that all viewpoints, especially those of extremists, are legitimate targets for satire. Herzog comments, "They never do anything to be controversial; they do things to be funny. Some people think Matt and Trey are Democrats, and some think they're Republicans. But if you look at the show, there's not anybody who remains unscathed."[63]

Parker and Stone's commitment to aiming their satire at all targets will no doubt continue to include Hollywood celebrities as well; they show no signs of mellowing out or softening their attitude on that front. For example, referring to two actors known for their outspoken liberal opinions, Stone comments,

> You have to laugh at Alec Baldwin when he gets political. You have to. He is an amazing actor, he may even be a great guy, but that [expletive] is funny. Sean Penn getting on TV on CNN and talking about politics, Sean Penn running around [disasters such as] Katrina and Haiti—that is funny. That's all. That's [expletive] funny. And we're going to make fun of you, Sean Penn.[64]

The most notorious incidents of controversy in the duo's careers are still those revolving around Scientology and the depiction of Muhammad. But there have been more recent incidents as well. For example, Parker and Stone found themselves inadvertently caught up in an international political firestorm late in 2014. This dramatic turn of events brought their decade-old puppet movie, 2004's *Team America*, back into the news.

The event was a cyberattack on a major Hollywood movie studio, Sony Pictures. The attack made public sensitive information from within the company, and it also wiped large amounts of data from the studio's system. The attackers announced that the assault had been made to stop the release of *The Interview*, a comedy about a plan to assassinate North Korea's unstable dictator Kim Jong Un.

Sony complied with this demand and withdrew the film from release. In protest, three independent theaters in Texas, Ohio, and Georgia announced that they would screen *Team America* instead. They pointed out that the earlier film had satirized Kim Jong Il, Kim Jong Un's father and predecessor. However, *Team America*'s studio, Paramount, refused to release Parker and Stone's film, so the three independent theaters were forced to cancel their plans. (Sony Pictures later reversed its decision and released *The Interview* across the country.) No

Parker and Stone sit among the marionettes and props used to create Team America: World Police. *In 2014, when Sony pulled* The Interview *from theaters in response to cyberthreats, theater owners wanted to screen the ten-year-old* Team America *as a replacement.*

matter how it played out, the controversy was good news for Parker and Stone: DVD sales of *Team America* skyrocketed in its aftermath.

Alongside their willingness to handle controversy that (intentionally or not) comes their way, Parker and Stone also remain committed to poking fun at anything and everything that also comes their way. All subjects are equally ripe for satire, they say, and therefore they refuse to take sides on any topic. Parker comments, "I look at it like this. I have a cat, I love my cat and it's like someone coming in and saying, 'Hey, is that cat a Republican or a Democrat?' He's my [expletive] cat, leave him alone."[65]

Arming Cartman

Parker and Stone had not set out to create controversy when the attack on Sony happened. Another example of the partners' unwitting involvement in controversy was a scandal that was revealed in 2010.

Employees of a private American security company, Blackwater, were caught supplying violent drug users in Afghanistan with weapons that were intended for the Afghan National Police. During the subsequent investigation it was revealed that someone in Blackwater had signed for several hundred of these weapons using the name Eric Cartman.

For their part, Parker and Stone were bemused by the incident. Parker said at the time that he was not angered by the use of his character's name, even for something like illegal weapon sales. He told a reporter, "It makes perfect sense. It's the name I would use. Our first reaction to any story is 'How do we put this into the show?' and the second reaction is 'Did Cartman do that?' because he's so real to us it's like 'I bet Cartman did that.'"[66]

A less inflammatory, ongoing controversy revolves around the question of illegal downloading from the Internet. It is common for musicians, filmmakers, and other artists to actively block such activity, which they see as stealing their work (and profits). But Parker and Stone insist that they are not concerned about fans "stealing" their shows. Stone comments, "We're always in favor of people downloading. Always. It's how a lot of people see the show. And it's never hurt us. We've done nothing but been successful with the show. How could you ever get mad about somebody who wants to see your stuff?"[67]

New Frontiers

The two say that they look forward to new frontiers of controversy in the future, whether it shows up on the Broadway stage, movie screens, television, or elsewhere. In any case, the partners point out, they will have to be increasingly outrageous.

They note that the boundaries of what is acceptable have changed dramatically in the years since *South Park* debuted. In fact, they assert, the show's early episodes seem positively tame by today's standards, both for their social commentary and their rude humor. Perhaps exaggerating a little, Parker claims, "When we look at the shows we were doing years ago—to think that people were freaking out over these episodes! If you look at our first season now, you could put it on PBS next to *Sesame Street*."[68]

Parker and Stone have frequently stated that their love of using rude humor in all of their projects has not changed as they have matured. Artistically, they admit, they are still the naughty boys they have always been. Asked by a reporter if *South Park* and its creators have changed much over the years, Parker replied, "I would love to say yes, but I don't think we've grown up. We're still basically doing fart jokes. Thanks for rubbing it in our face."[69]

"I don't think we've grown up. We're still basically doing fart jokes."[69]

—Trey Parker.

This flippant attitude has served Parker and Stone well. For one thing, they are extremely rich and famous. (Stone half jokingly remarks, "Basically all we've ever done is said what we wanted to say, and people have just thrown money at us."[70]) They have been artistically successful as well, thanks in large part to their gift for using offensive jokes to create some of the most incisive and funniest satire around. As a result, journalist David Carr notes that "life is pretty good when you never grow up."[71] And maybe Parker and Stone never will.

SOURCE NOTES

Introduction: Welcome to Trey and Matt's World

1. Carl Swanson, "Latter-Day Saints," *New York*, March 7, 2011. http://nymag.com.
2. David R. Koepsell, "They Satirized My Prophet . . . ," in *"South Park" and Philosophy: You Know, I Learned Something Today,* ed. Robert Arp. Malden, MA: Blackwell, 2007, p. 131.
3. Quoted in Nick Gillespie and Jesse Walker, "*South Park* Libertarians," *Reason*, December 2006. http://reason.com.
4. Gillespie and Walker, "*South Park* Libertarians."

Chapter One: From Colorado to LA

5. Quoted in David Wild, "*South Park*'s Evil Geniuses," *Rolling Stone*, February 19, 1998. www.rollingstone.com.
6. Quoted in Gavin Haynes, "A Moron's Guide to Trey Parker," VICE, March 13, 2013. www.vice.com.
7. Quoted in Steve Pond, "The *Playboy* Interview: Trey Parker and Matt Stone," *Playboy* (Kindle edition), June 2000.
8. Quoted in Wild, "*South Park*'s Evil Geniuses."
9. Quoted in Pond, "The *Playboy* Interview."
10. Quoted in Wild, "*South Park*'s Evil Geniuses."
11. Quoted in Gillespie and Walker, "*South Park* Libertarians."
12. Quoted in Wild, "*South Park*'s Evil Geniuses."
13. Quoted in David Chute, "Will 'Cannibal! The Musical' Be the Next 'Rocky Horror'?," *Los Angeles Times*, June 5, 1998. http://articles.latimes.com.
14. Quoted in MTV, "About Trey Parker." www.mtv.com.
15. Quoted in Wild, "*South Park*'s Evil Geniuses."

16. Quoted in ZAP2It, "'South Park' Creator Trey Parker Cops to Kooky Universal Spoof," July 16, 2001. http://treyparker.info.

Chapter Two: Creating *South Park*

17. Quoted in Jasper Rees, "Where Seinfeld's a Turkey," *Independent* (London), June 15, 1998. www.independent.co.uk.
18. Quoted in Alex Leo, "Matt Stone & Trey Parker Are Not Your Political Allies (No Matter What You Believe)," *Huffington Post*, April 27, 2010. www.huffingtonpost.com.
19. Quoted in Wild, "*South Park*'s Evil Geniuses."
20. Quoted in Wild, "*South Park*'s Evil Geniuses."
21. Henry Jacoby, "You Know, I Learned Something Today," in *"South Park" and Philosophy: You Know, I Learned Something Today,* ed. Robert Arp. Malden, MA: Blackwell, 2007, p. 57.
22. Quoted in Rees, "Where Seinfeld's a Turkey."
23. Devin Leonard, "'South Park' Creators Haven't Lost Their Edge," *Fortune*, October 27, 2006. http://archive.fortune.com.
24. Quoted in Leonard, "'South Park' Creators Haven't Lost Their Edge."
25. Stephanie Zacharek, "*South Park: Bigger, Longer & Uncut*," *Salon*, July 2, 1999. www.salon.com.
26. Quoted in Leonard, "'South Park' Creators Haven't Lost Their Edge."
27. Quoted in Mychelle Vasvary, "Exclusive Interview with Anne Garefino," *Morton Report*, July 20, 2011. www.themortonreport.com.
28. Quoted in James Hibberd, "'South Park' Blows Deadline for First Time Ever," *Entertainment Weekly*, October 16, 2013. http://insidetv.ew.com.
29. Quoted in Pond, "The *Playboy* Interview."

30. Quoted in Hibberd, "'South Park' Blows Deadline for First Time Ever."

31. Quoted in Gillespie and Walker, "*South Park* Libertarians."

32. Quoted in Gillespie and Walker, "*South Park* Libertarians."

Chapter Three: Win Some, Lose Some

33. Quoted in Roger Ebert, "*Orgazmo*," RogerEbert.com, October 23, 1998. www.rogerebert.com.

34. Quoted in *The South Park Scriptorium* 1991–1999. www.spscriptorium.com.

35. Zacharek, "*South Park.*"

36. Rita Kempley, "The Wickedly Funny 'South Park,'" *Washington Post*, June 30, 1999. www.washingtonpost.com.

37. Quoted in Gillespie and Walker, "*South Park* Libertarians."

38. Quoted in Contactmusic.com, "Parker and Stone Suffered on Set," January 10, 2005. http://hub.contactmusic.com.

39. Quoted in RedEye Staff, "Puppetry of Politics," *Chicago Tribune*, August 5, 2004. http://articles.chicagotribune.com.

40. David Itzkoff, "A Sweet Show, with Blasphemy and Cussing," *New York Times*, February 16, 2011. www.nytimes.com.

41. Quoted in Itzkoff, "A Sweet Show, with Blasphemy and Cussing."

42. Quoted in Gillespie and Walker, "*South Park* Libertarians."

43. Quoted in Stephen Galloway, "The Bad Boys of 'South Park' Grow Up," *Hollywood Reporter*, March 22, 2011. www.hollywoodreporter.com.

44. Quoted in Itzkoff, "A Sweet Show, with Blasphemy and Cussing."

Chapter Four: *Now* What?

45. Quoted in *Vanity Fair*, "The New Establishment 2013," November 2013. www.vanityfair.com.

46. Quoted in Ross Sorkin and Amy Chozik, "'South Park' Creators to Start Company, Important Studios," *New York Times*, January 13, 2013. www.nytimes.com.

47. Quoted in Wild, "*South Park*'s Evil Geniuses."

48. Quoted in Stephen Galloway, "Why *South Park*'s Trey Parker and Matt Stone Now Say It's 'Wrong' to Offend," *Hollywood Reporter*, March 24, 2011. www.hollywoodreporter.com.

49. Quoted in Carl Swanson, "Latter-Day Saints," *New York*, March 7, 2011. http://nymag.com.

50. Quoted in Swanson, "Latter-Day Saints."

51. Quoted in Pond, "The *Playboy* Interview."

52. Quoted in Wild, "*South Park*'s Evil Geniuses."

53. Quoted in Pond, "The *Playboy* Interview."

54. Swanson, "Latter-Day Saints."

55. Quoted in Galloway, "Why *South Park*'s Trey Parker and Matt Stone Now Say It's 'Wrong' to Offend."

56. Quoted in Heather Havrilesky, "Puppet Masters," *Guardian* (Manchester), October 12, 2004. www.theguardian.com.

57. Quoted in David Carr, "'South Park' Marches On in New Places," *New York Times*, July 12, 2014. www.nytimes.com.

58. Quoted in Gillespie and Walker, "*South Park* Libertarians."

59. Quoted in Sorkin and Chozik, "'South Park' Creators to Start Company, Important Studios."

60. Quoted in Lisa Rose, "Former Ween Member Mickey Melchiondo Sets Sights on Reality TV Stardom," *Newark Star-Ledger*, January 24, 2014. www.nj.com.

61. Quoted in Pond, "The *Playboy* Interview."

62. Quoted in Pond, "The *Playboy* Interview."

63. Quoted in Swanson, "Latter-Day Saints."

64. Quoted in Leo, "Matt Stone & Trey Parker Are Not Your Political Allies."

65. Quoted in Leo, "Matt Stone & Trey Parker Are Not Your Political Allies."

66. Quoted in Leo, "Matt Stone & Trey Parker Are Not Your Political Allies."

67. Quoted in Gillespie and Walker, "*South Park* Libertarians."

68. Quoted in Gillespie and Walker, "*South Park* Libertarians."

69. Quoted in Terry Gross, "Making Fun of Everyone on 'South Park.'" *Fresh Air* (National Public Radio), March 24, 2010. www.npr.org.

70. Quoted in Gillespie and Walker, "*South Park* Libertarians."

71. Carr, "'South Park' Marches On in New Places."

IMPORTANT EVENTS IN THE LIVES OF TREY PARKER AND MATT STONE

1969
Randolph Severn Parker III is born on October 19 in Conifer, Colorado.

1971
Matthew Richard Stone is born May 26 in Houston, Texas.

1989
Parker and Stone meet at the University of Colorado in Boulder.

1992
Parker and Stone, who had made many short films together, create *Jesus vs. Frosty*, a short that is a direct predecessor of *South Park.*

1993
The pair's first feature-length film, *Alferd Packer: The Musical*, debuts at a movie theater in Boulder.

1994
Parker and Stone move to Los Angeles.

1995
Parker and Stone produce *The Spirit of Christmas,* a short that becomes one of the first videos to go viral.

1995–1996
Parker and Stone begin work on developing *South Park.*

1997
South Park's first season debuts and immediately becomes Comedy Central's top show.

1999
South Park: Bigger, Longer & Uncut is released.

2004
Team America: World Police is released.

2005
A *South Park* episode about Scientology causes a major controversy.

2006
South Park airs two episodes in which the Prophet Muhammad appears but causes relatively little controversy.

2010
A second set of shows about Muhammad sparks major worldwide controversy and threats of violence.

2011
Parker and Stone's musical, *The Book of Mormon*, debuts on Broadway.

2013
Parker and Stone form Important Studios, an independent production facility for film, TV, and other projects.

2014
Team America is in the news again as part of a controversy over the cyberhacking of Sony Pictures, apparently by North Korea.

2015
South Park's contract is renewed through at least 2016.

FOR FURTHER RESEARCH

Books

Matt Stone and Trey Parker, *The "South Park" Guide to Life*. Philadelphia: Running, 2009.

Matt Stone and Trey Parker, *The "South Park" Kit: Dude, Sweet!* Philadelphia: Running, 2009.

Dave Thompson, *South Park FAQ: All That's Left to Know About the Who, What, Where, When, and #%$* of America's Favorite Mountain Town*. New York: Applause, 2014.

Websites

Huffington Post, "Huff Post *South Park*" (www.huffingtonpost.com/news/south-park). A gateway to many articles about *South Park* on the journal's site.

South Park (southpark.cc.com). The official website of the show, maintained by Comedy Central, with free streaming episodes, blogs, news, and more.

SP Studio (www.sp-studio.de). A hilarious site maintained by a German graphic designer that lets you design your own cartoon character.

Wikia, "South Park Archives," (http://southpark.wikia.com/wiki/South_Park_Archives). A source for character descriptions, episode synopses, and more.

WikiHow, "How to Play BASEketball" (www.wikihow.com/Play-Baseketball). A description of and rules for the ridiculous invented game in the movie of the same title.

Video

"Cannibal: The Musical . . . Trailer" (www.youtube.com/watch?v=8GszhYsV3MM). The trailer for the fake musical that Parker and Stone made while film students at the University of Colorado.

"Man on Mars" (www.youtube.com/watch?v=2FczN5PI0zQ). A live-action short that Parker and Stone created as college film students.

"The Spirit of Christmas" (also known as "Jesus vs. Santa") (www.youtube.com/watch?v=gOYVlRHuymc). A short that marked the first appearance in their final form of South Park's main characters.

"Your Studio and You" (www.youtube.com/watch?v=IN7CZZryUNU). The hilarious fake documentary, filled with cameos by famous actors and directors, that Parker and Stone created to spoof Universal Studios.

Note: Boldface page numbers indicate illustrations.

PICTURE CREDITS

Cover: © RD/Orchon/Retna, Ltd./Corbis

Associated Press, 43, 47, 57

Depositphotos, 8

© Mitchell Gerber/Corbis, 21

Graylock/ABACAUSA.COM/Newscom, 30

KUSUI ENTERPRISES/Album/Newscom, 38

Michel iPhoto Inc./Newscom, 53

Photofest Images, 13, 18, 24, 32, 62

ABOUT THE AUTHOR

Adam Woog has written many books for adults, young adults, and children as well as a monthly books column for the *Seattle Times*. He is also a preschool teacher. Woog lives in Seattle, Washington, with his wife, and they have a grown daughter.